What Makes Princess Diana Special?

BIOGRAPHY OF FAMOUS PEOPLE

Children's Biography Books

DISSECTED LIVES
auto biographies

Speedy Publishing LLC

40 E. Main St. #1156

Newark, DE 19711

www.speedypublishing.com

Copyright 2017

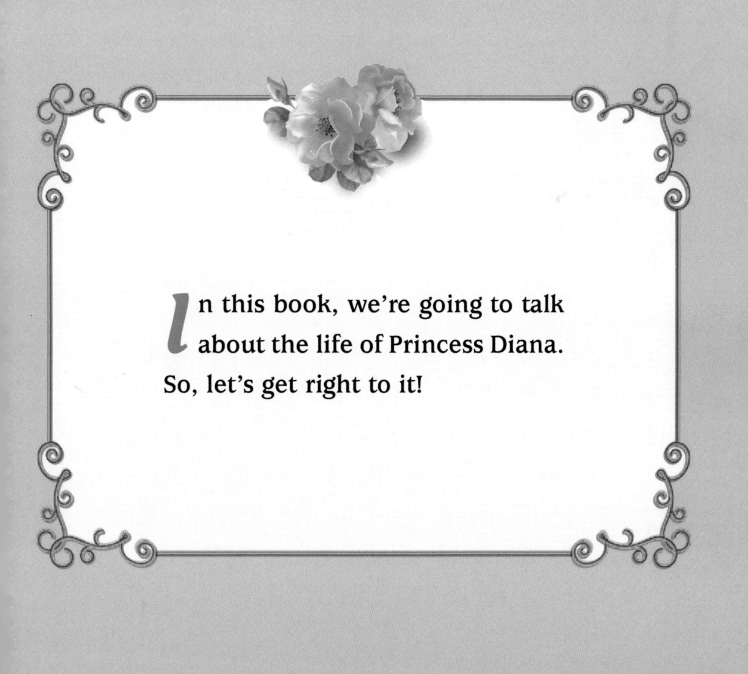

In this book, we're going to talk about the life of Princess Diana. So, let's get right to it!

WHO WAS PRINCESS DIANA?

Princess Diana was Prince Charles's first wife. He is the heir to the British throne and is the son of Queen Elizabeth II. Because of her warmth and humanitarian efforts, Princess Diana was one of the most loved members of the royal family. Sadly, she died in a car crash in 1997. She was only 36 years old when she passed away.

PRINCESS DIANA

ALTHORP HOUSE,
NORTHAMPTONSHIRE

DIANA'S EARLY LIFE

Princess Diana was born on the first of July in 1961 in England near the city of Sandringham. Her parents were Edward John Spencer known as the Viscount Althorp and Frances Ruth Burke Roche known as the Viscountess Althorp.

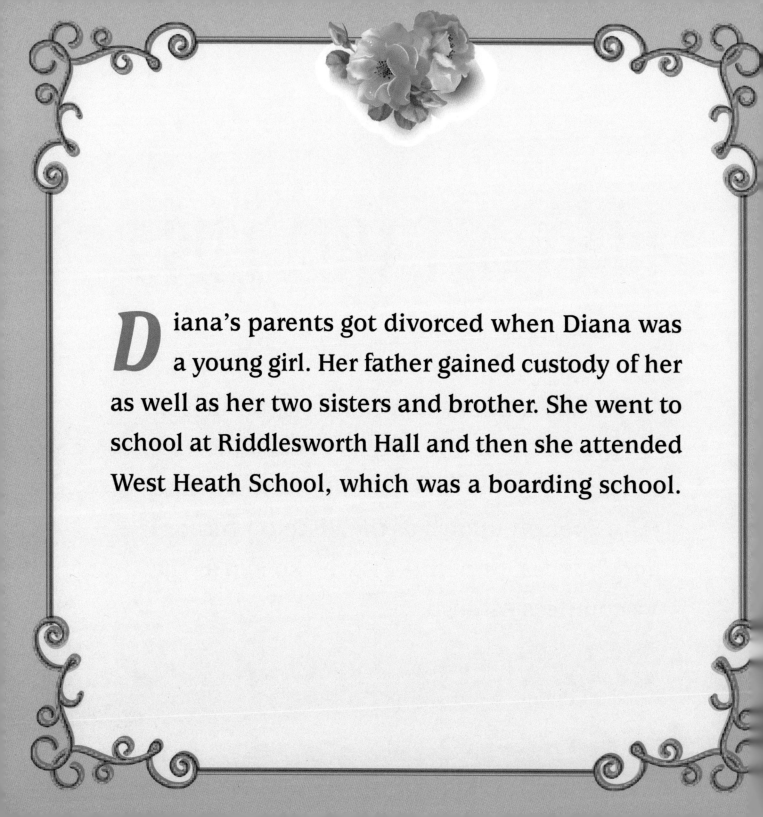

Diana's parents got divorced when Diana was a young girl. Her father gained custody of her as well as her two sisters and brother. She went to school at Riddlesworth Hall and then she attended West Heath School, which was a boarding school.

RIDDLESWORTH HALL

YOUNG PRINCESS DIANA

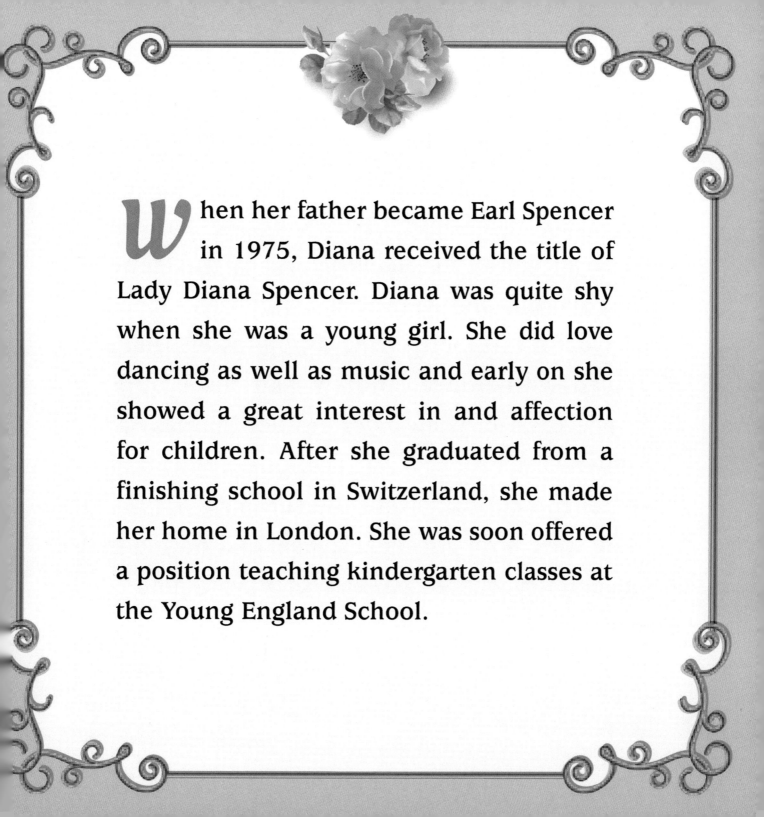

When her father became Earl Spencer in 1975, Diana received the title of Lady Diana Spencer. Diana was quite shy when she was a young girl. She did love dancing as well as music and early on she showed a great interest in and affection for children. After she graduated from a finishing school in Switzerland, she made her home in London. She was soon offered a position teaching kindergarten classes at the Young England School.

The Spencer family had been close with the royal family for many years. At that time, they were living in a house that was owned by Queen Elizabeth II. As a youngster, Diana played with Prince Andrew and his brother Prince Edward. Their older brother Charles had known Diana for several years but didn't think of her romantically until the summer of 1980. They were both guests at a weekend outing in the country where Charles was playing polo.

PRINCE CHARLES

BALMORAL CASTLE

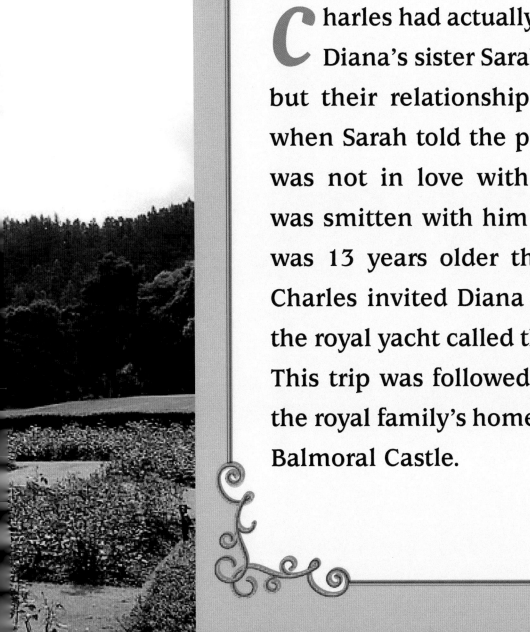

Charles had actually been dating Diana's sister Sarah for a while, but their relationship went south when Sarah told the press that she was not in love with him. Diana was smitten with him although he was 13 years older than she was. Charles invited Diana for a trip on the royal yacht called the Britannia. This trip was followed by a visit to the royal family's home in Scotland, Balmoral Castle.

There, Diana was more formally introduced to Charles's mother Queen Elizabeth II, his father, Prince Philip, and his grandmother, the Queen Mother. This visit went well and then the couple dated in London.

After a quick 6-month courtship, Prince Charles asked Diana to marry him. She was in love with him, but he professed later that he was never in love with her.

PRINCE CHARLES AND PRINCESS DIANA

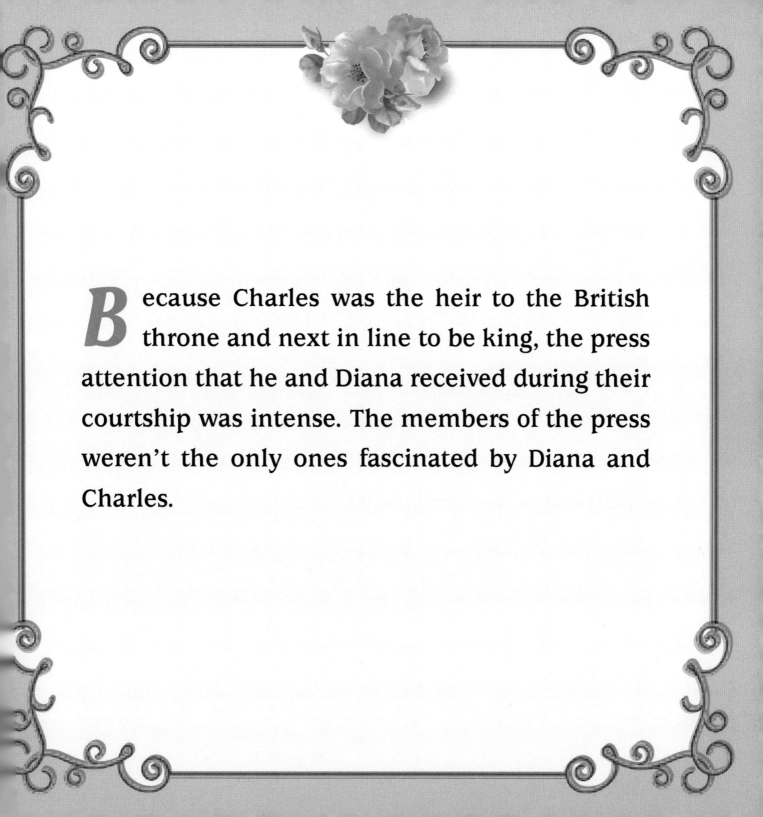

*B*ecause Charles was the heir to the British throne and next in line to be king, the press attention that he and Diana received during their courtship was intense. The members of the press weren't the only ones fascinated by Diana and Charles.

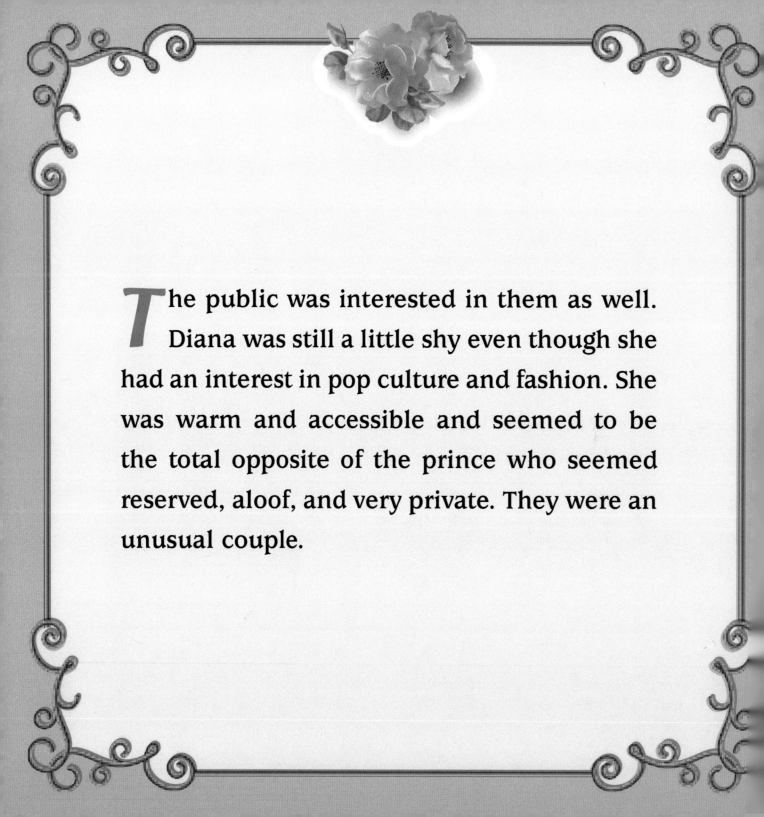

The public was interested in them as well. Diana was still a little shy even though she had an interest in pop culture and fashion. She was warm and accessible and seemed to be the total opposite of the prince who seemed reserved, aloof, and very private. They were an unusual couple.

PRINCESS DIANA

PRINCESS DIANA AND PRINCE CHARLES WEDDING

CHARLES AND DIANA MARRY

Charles and Diana were married on the 29th of July in 1981. Their wedding was shown on television and millions of people around the world watched their fairy tale ceremony. In June of 1982, their first son was born and they named him William Arthur. Two years later, they had their second son, Henry Charles, who was nicknamed "Harry." Charles and Diana loved their sons, but their marriage wasn't happy.

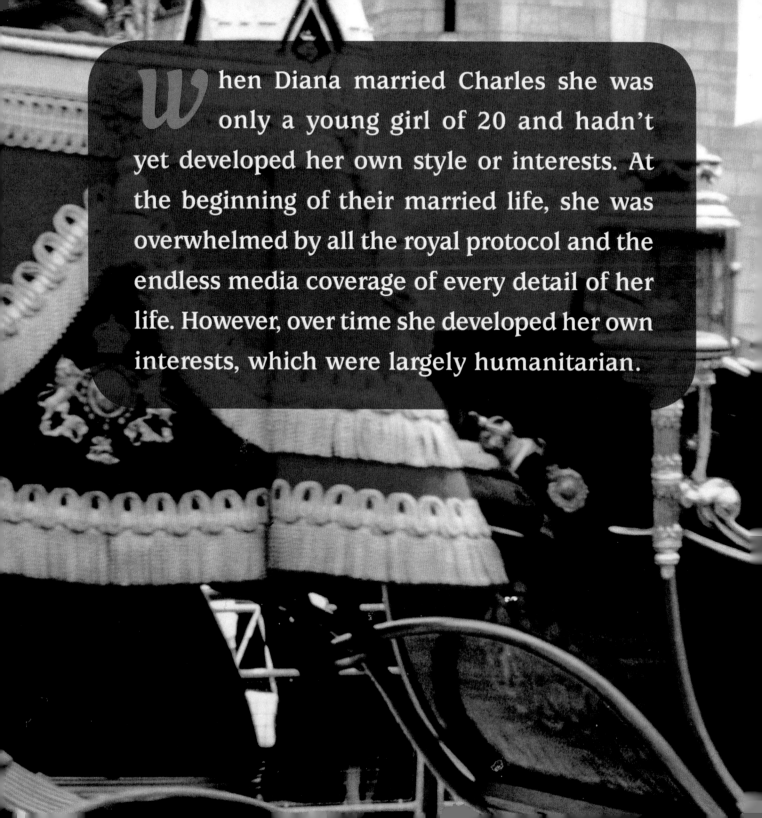

When Diana married Charles she was only a young girl of 20 and hadn't yet developed her own style or interests. At the beginning of their married life, she was overwhelmed by all the royal protocol and the endless media coverage of every detail of her life. However, over time she developed her own interests, which were largely humanitarian.

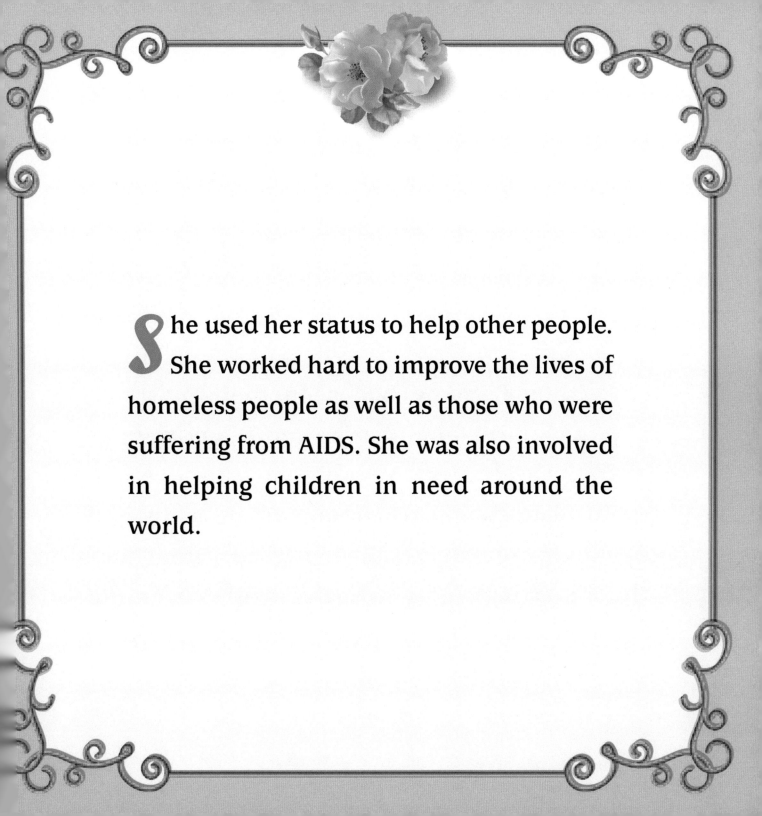

She used her status to help other people. She worked hard to improve the lives of homeless people as well as those who were suffering from AIDS. She was also involved in helping children in need around the world.

CHARLES AND DIANA DIVORCE

Although many had seen their marriage as a fairy tale, Charles and Diana weren't "happily-ever-after." After eleven years together, their relationship was coming apart. Diana had been very unhappy and depressed throughout their marriage. She struggled with an eating disorder called bulimia and other types of self-destructive behaviors.

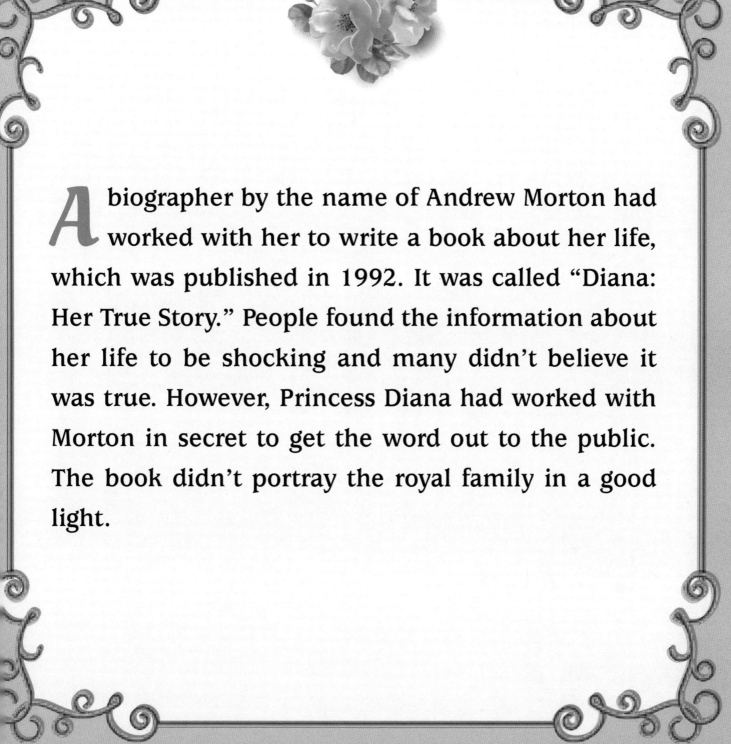

A biographer by the name of Andrew Morton had worked with her to write a book about her life, which was published in 1992. It was called "Diana: Her True Story." People found the information about her life to be shocking and many didn't believe it was true. However, Princess Diana had worked with Morton in secret to get the word out to the public. The book didn't portray the royal family in a good light.

*I*n December of 1992, there was a formal announcement from John Major, the Prime Minister, stating that Charles and Diana were going to separate. The separation placed Diana in an awkward situation. Although her sons were in line for the throne, she wouldn't be considered a member of the royal family anymore.

A NEED FOR PRIVACY

*T*hroughout her marriage, Diana had always been in the public eye and tabloid photographers were always taking photos of her and her children. She desperately wanted to have some privacy. In December of 1993, she stated that she was going to step out of the spotlight for a while. She wanted a normal life.

*T*hinking that she would have more privacy, she gave up her police security protection in 1994. Unfortunately, it didn't have the desired effect. The tabloid photographers, called paparazzi, went after her and her children even more than before. They followed her wherever she went right up until the night of her tragic car accident.

PRINCE CHARLES

PRINCE CHARLES'S REPUTATION

The biography that had been written about Diana's life and their marital problems didn't help Prince Charles's reputation. In 1994, a film documentary about Charles was created and aired. In the documentary, which celebrated his 25th anniversary as Prince of Wales, Charles made it seem that the problems they had were largely due to Diana's mental troubles.

THE SECRET TELEVISION INTERVIEW

Diana decided that she would tell the British people and the world about what she'd gone through during her marriage. Many of her friends and associates advised her not to do this because the royal family would get very upset.

GREAT BRITAIN VIEWED THE PROGRAM

However, Diana arranged for the secret television interview and didn't tell the royal family what she was doing until a week before the program was scheduled to go on the air. The program aired on November 20, 1995 and Diana was very candid about her life and problems. Over 23 million viewers in Great Britain viewed the program and it was broadcast worldwide.

THE QUEEN WRITES A LETTER

About a month after the program aired, Queen Elizabeth wrote a letter to Diana and Charles to recommend that they go forward with a formal divorce. Diana would share custody of her children with Charles and she received a sum of 17 million pounds, but she wasn't a member of the royal family anymore.

QUEEN ELIZABETH II

HUMANITARIAN CAUSES

Diana continued to work for the many causes she was involved with after her divorce in 1996. She went to the country of Angola to bring worldwide attention to the landmines. The landmines were still exploding well after the civil war in the country had ended. On the trip, she visited with the victims of landmine explosions.

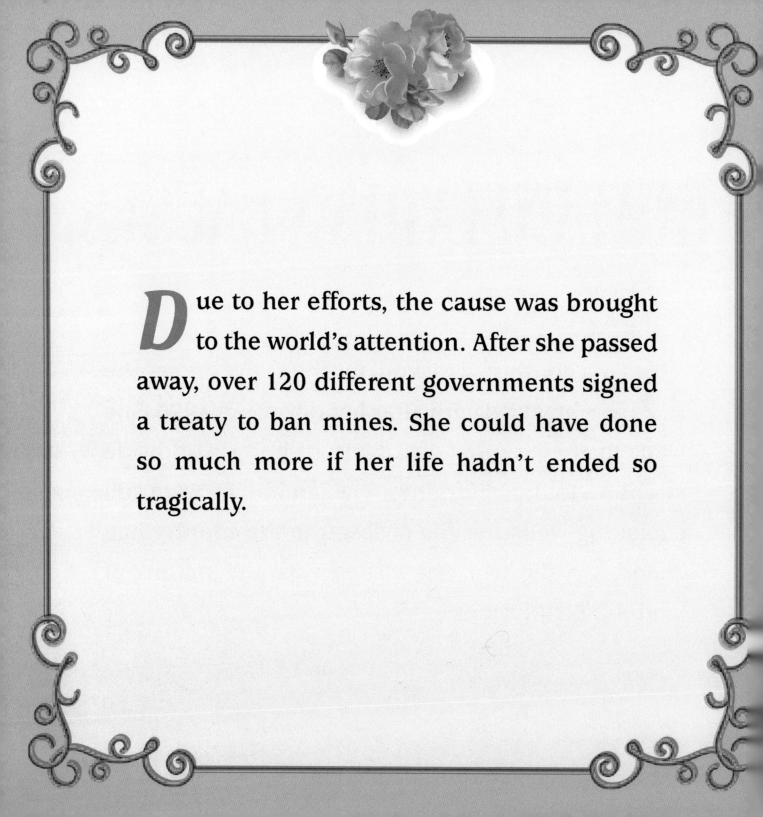

Due to her efforts, the cause was brought to the world's attention. After she passed away, over 120 different governments signed a treaty to ban mines. She could have done so much more if her life hadn't ended so tragically.

It's Over

Diana and Charles are history, but a battle royal looms over her future

FLOWERS FOR PINCESS DIANA

DIANA'S DEATH

She was visiting Paris with her new boyfriend Dodi Al-Fayed, a film producer from Egypt, when tragedy struck. They were trying to drive away from tabloid photographers when their car crashed on the 30th of August 1997.

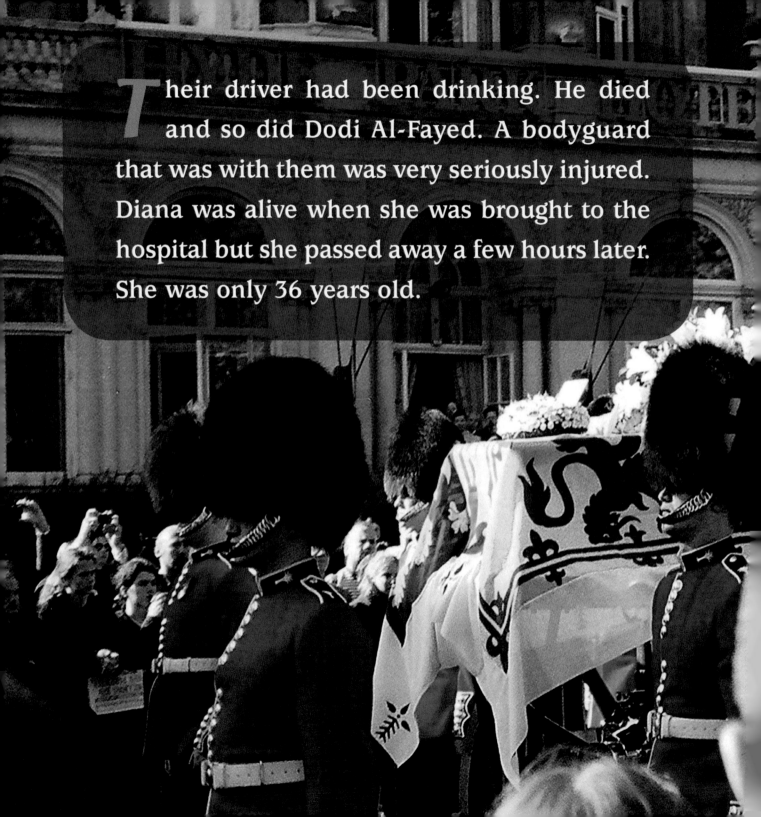

Their driver had been drinking. He died and so did Dodi Al-Fayed. A bodyguard that was with them was very seriously injured. Diana was alive when she was brought to the hospital but she passed away a few hours later. She was only 36 years old.

PRINCESS DIANA'S FUNERAL

WHY DID THE WORLD LOVE DIANA?

Princess Diana was popular in her own country and around the world. She was a beautiful woman who transformed from a shy young girl to a fashionable, trend-setting member of royalty. She was a loving mother and cared deeply about her own sons as well as about the fate of children everywhere.

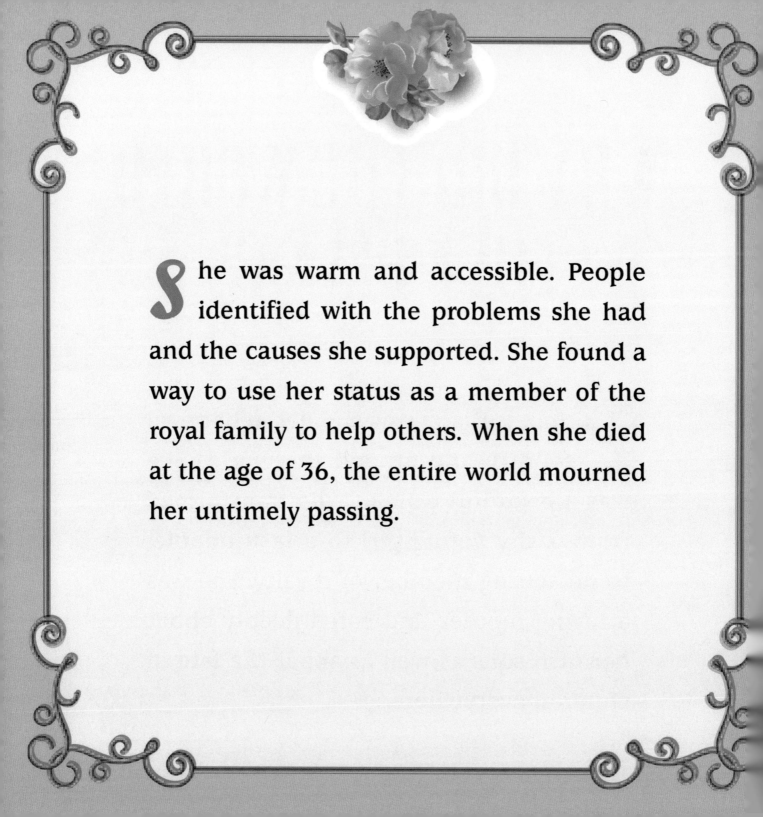

She was warm and accessible. People identified with the problems she had and the causes she supported. She found a way to use her status as a member of the royal family to help others. When she died at the age of 36, the entire world mourned her untimely passing.

Diana, Princess of Wales
(1961-1997)

$300

Diana, Princess of Wales

Guyana

t made the late Princess Diana so easy to love was not her eternal beauty, her fashionable
othing, her international appearances or her time spent on charitable causes. It was her
an qualities as a Mother of two Children and as an independent, modern woman that gave
world an upscale ambassador who they could relate to and understand on their own level.
he will forever be remembered as the People's Princess and the Queen of People's hearts.

Rundo

THE PEOPLE'S PRINCESS

When Diana Spencer married Prince Charles she became Princess of Wales in 1981. They had two sons, William and Harry, who were heirs to the throne after their father. Princess Diana was a beautiful, warm person who truly cared about others. She used her status as a royal to further humanitarian causes and the world mourned her tragic death in 1997.

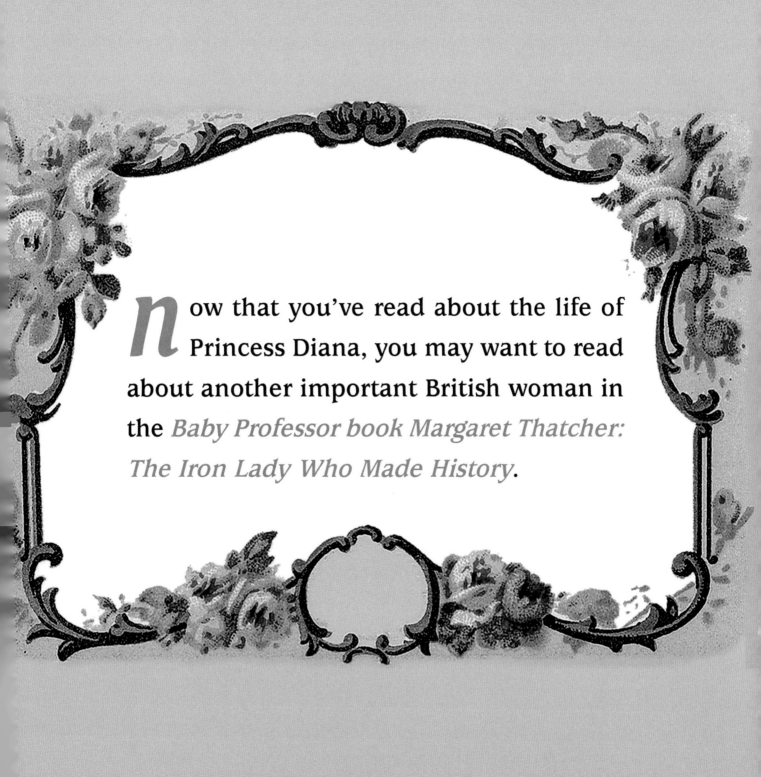

n ow that you've read about the life of Princess Diana, you may want to read about another important British woman in the *Baby Professor book Margaret Thatcher: The Iron Lady Who Made History*.

Visit

DISSECTED LIVES
auto biographies

www.DissectedLives.Com

To download more inspiring autobiographies and biographies
of great people from our website. Discover more about people
that changed the world during their time!

Visit our website to download more
Free eBooks and Get Discount Codes!

Made in the USA
San Bernardino, CA
18 May 2020